LEARN TO PLAY THE ALFI
RECORDER

by Morton Manus

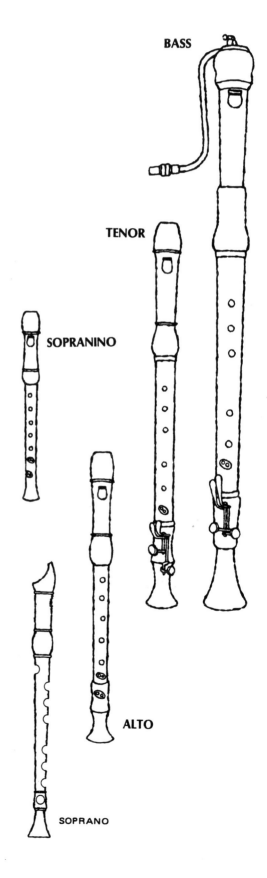

The Recorder Family

There are six members of the recorder family: the Sopranino, the Soprano, the Alto, the Tenor, the Bass and the Big Bass. Of these, four are more popular and in general use:

THE SOPRANO (or Descant) is about 12½ inches long and is the leading melody instrument. It is pitched in C and the notes are written an octave (eight notes) lower than they sound.

THE ALTO (sometimes called the Treble) is about 18½ inches long and is the principal instrument of the entire family. It is an F instrument with the notes written as they sound. It is considered the traditional instrument for which many of the great masters (Bach, Handel, Purcell, etc.) wrote their Sonatas.

THE TENOR is pitched in C and is about 25½ inches long. The notes are written as they sound. It is a melody instrument that is often used in ensemble playing.

THE BASS is pitched in F and is about 36 inches long. It is primarily an ensemble instrument. The notes are written as they sound and the range is an octave lower than the Alto.

The two lesser used instruments are the:

BIG BASS, pitched in C, sounds an octave lower than the Tenor. It is about 49 inches long, is wider than the Bass and has a larger and richer tone.

THE SOPRANINO, 9 inches long, is the smallest in size and highest in pitch. It is an F instrument and the notes, like the Soprano, are written one octave lower than they sound.

Preface

This method for the Recorder (sometimes called English Flute) is designed to give quick, practical and interesting instruction on the Soprano, Tenor, and the rather rare Big Bass Recorders. The building of finger technique and tonguing is done through music, rather than the dry repetition of monotonous exercises. In this method, you will find the greatest variety of folk songs, sacred and Christmas music, hymns and jigs, plus many of the lighter works of the great masters.

HOW TO HOLD THE RECORDER

Your first concern will be the position of the left hand as all the fingerings in the beginning are with the left hand. Hold the Recorder so that the center of the 1st finger of the left hand covers the hole nearest the mouthpiece. Do not attempt to cover the hole with just the tip of the finger. Keep the fingers as flat as possible, with the left thumb covering the hole on the back of the instrument. The 2nd finger covers the 2nd hole; the 3rd finger covers the 3rd hole. The 4th finger of the left hand is not used. Hold the mouthpiece between the lips only; do not bite the tip of the mouthpiece. Put no more than a half-inch of the mouthpiece into your mouth.

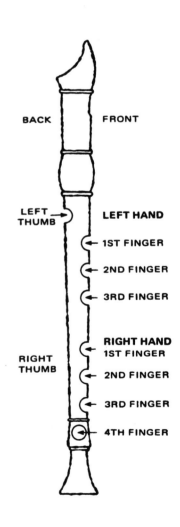

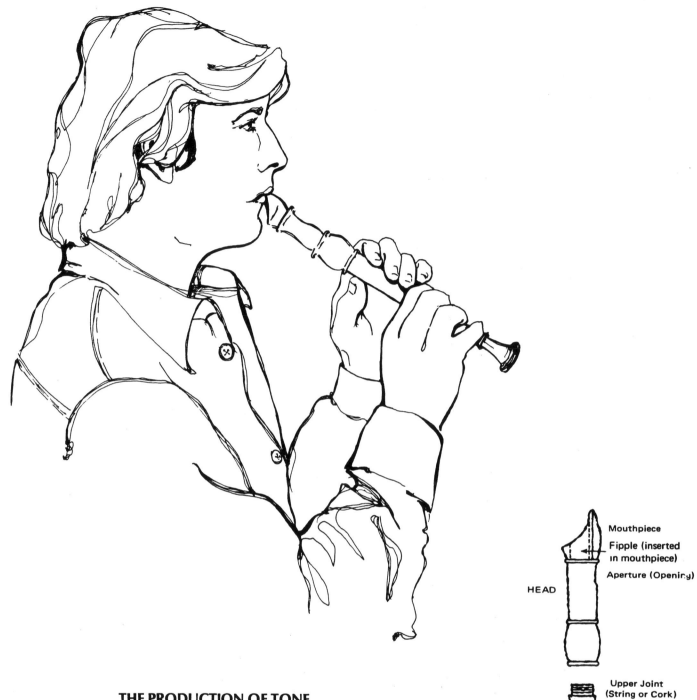

THE PRODUCTION OF TONE

It is important not to overblow, that is, not to blow too hard. Until you develop control of the tonguing, play softly. Most teachers advocate the use of "du" to tongue the low notes and "tu" for the high notes. For the first few days, play a little each day rather than a long session one day and nothing the next. As you progress in tone and technique, make the playing periods longer.

CARE OF THE RECORDER

If your Recorder is made of wood, warm it with the hands before playing. Begin your first studies with short periods. When you are through playing, be sure to dry the instrument with a swab. If you assemble your new Recorder, be very gentle in putting the sections together. The Recorder is a delicate instrument and any force can crack it. If necessary, apply a little cork grease on the tight-fitting joints.

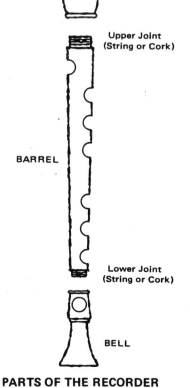

Mouthpiece
Fipple (inserted in mouthpiece)
Aperture (Opening)
HEAD
Upper Joint (String or Cork)
BARREL
Lower Joint (String or Cork)
BELL

PARTS OF THE RECORDER

Getting acquainted with music

NOTES — Musical sounds are indicated by symbols called NOTES. Their time value is determined by their color (white or black) and by stems and flags attached to the note:

THE STAFF — The notes are named after the first seven letters of the alphabet (A to G), endlessly repeated to include the entire range of musical sound. The name and pitch of the note is indicated by its position on five horizontal lines and the spaces between, which is called the staff.

————— 5th LINE —————	
	4th SPACE
————— 4th LINE —————	
	3rd SPACE
————— 3rd LINE —————	
	2nd SPACE
————— 2nd LINE —————	
	1st SPACE
————— 1st LINE —————	

NOTES ON THE LINES   NOTES IN THE SPACES

THE TREBLE CLEF — The TREBLE CLEF was originally written as the letter G because it was used to give the location of the G note on the staff. As it was always used to indicate the highest notes, it was called the Treble (which means the highest) or G Clef.

Treble or
G Clef

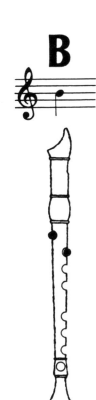

LET'S PLAY WITH B

The black notes with a stem up or down, are QUARTER NOTES.
They receive one beat (one count). Blow a gentle "Tu" on each note.

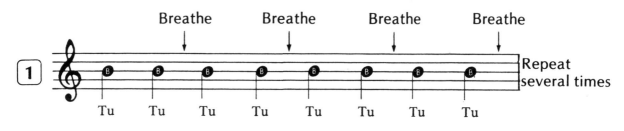

This ⸙ is a QUARTER REST. It is a sign of silence for one beat.

LET'S PLAY WITH A

AND AWAY WE GO

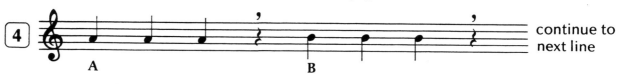

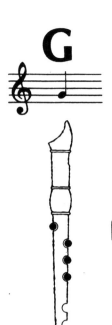

AND DOWN TO G

1   Repeat

MEASURES

Music is divided into equal parts called measures.
A bar line divides one measure from another.

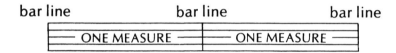

bar line   bar line   bar line

| ONE MEASURE | ONE MEASURE |

MERRILY

2   Play evenly

Mer - ri - ly we roll a - long, roll a - long, roll a - long,

3

Mer - ri - ly we roll a - long, on the deep blue sea.

AT THE FAIR

4   Play evenly

5

THE TIME SIGNATURE

At the beginning of every piece there are two numbers, called the *time signature*. The time signature tells the number of beats to each note and the number of beats in each measure.

2 ← The top number tells how many beats in each measure.

4 ← The bottom number tells us what kind of note gets one beat.

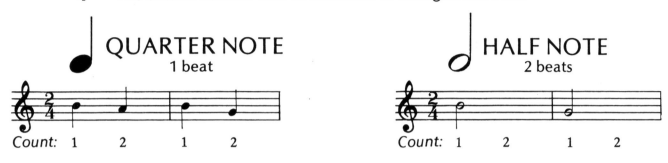

AU CLAIR DE LA LUNE

THREE BLIND MICE

(Duet = Two Parts — One person plays (a) part; another plays (b) part.)

Double bar line means the end of the piece.

When playing duets, alternate parts for additional practice.

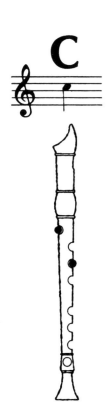

UP TO MIDDLE **C**

HAPPY NEW YEAR

(Duet)

A NEW TIME SIGNATURE

3 means three beats in a measure.

4 one beat for each quarter note.

Dotted half note gets three beats

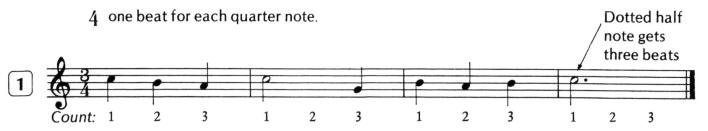

Count: 1 2 3 1 2 3 1 2 3 1 2 3

RIDDLE SONG

LIVERPOOL CHANTEY

ANOTHER TIME SIGNATURE

$\frac{4}{4}$ means four beats in a measure,
one beat for each quarter note.

Whole note gets four beats

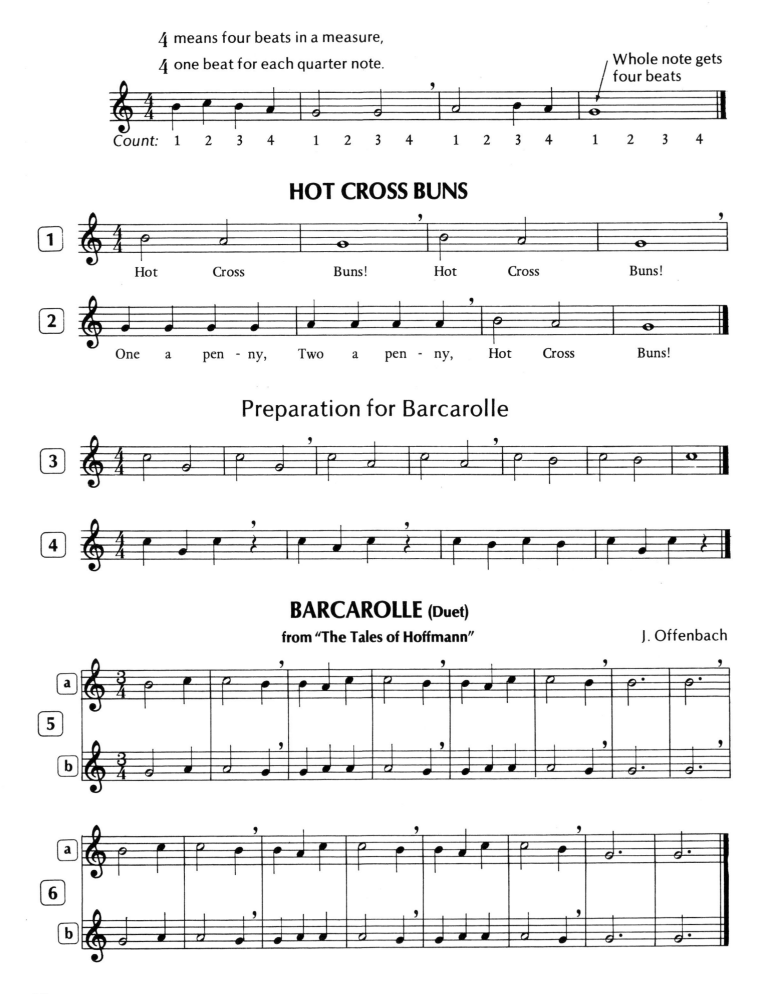

Count: 1 2 3 4 1 2 3 4 1 2 3 4 1 2 3 4

HOT CROSS BUNS

1 Hot   Cross   Buns!   Hot   Cross   Buns!

2 One   a   pen - ny,   Two   a   pen - ny,   Hot   Cross   Buns!

Preparation for Barcarolle

3

4

BARCAROLLE (Duet)
from "The Tales of Hoffmann"

J. Offenbach

5 a
  b

6 a
  b

10

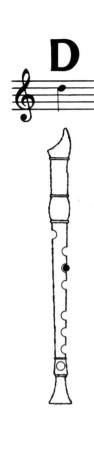

UP TO HIGH **D**

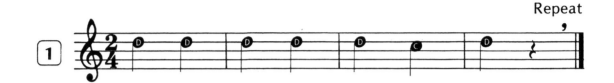

I KNOW WHERE I'M GOING

I know where I'm go - ing, I know who's go - ing with me;

I know who I love, And he knows who I'll mar - ry!

Feath - er beds are soft, And paint - ed rooms are bon - ny, But

I would trade them all, for strong and hand - some John - ny.

11.

GO TELL AUNT RHODY

Go   tell   Aunt   Rho - dy,   go   tell   Aunt   Rho - dy,

Go   tell   Aunt   Rho - dy the   old   gray   goose   is   dead.

AURA LEE
(Duet)

As   the   black - bird   in   the   Spring,   'Neath the   wil - low   tree,

Joy - ous - ly   I   heard him   sing   of   his   Au - ra   Lee.

Rhythm-E-Tick

Add up the total number of beats, then write the total in each square.

JINGLE BELLS
(Duet)

GOOD KING WENCESLAS
(Duet)

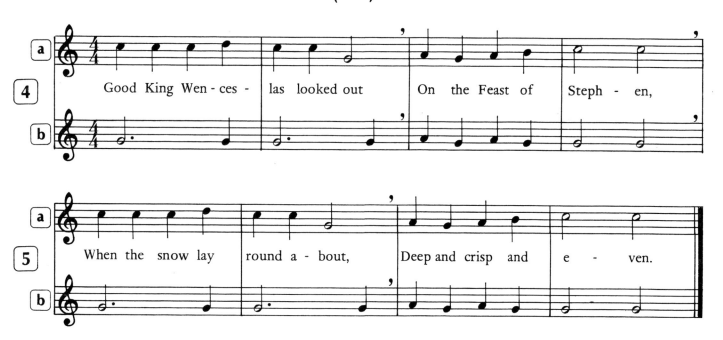

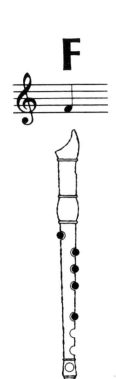

AND NOW TO LOW F

The double dots inside the double bars indicate that everything between the double bars must be repeated.

EXERCISE IN LEAPS

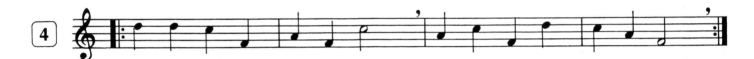

CANON

A Canon is a composition of two or more "parts" or voices, each voice in turn taking up the same melody (called the subject) and when combined, sound in harmony.

EIGHTH NOTES

Eighth notes are the black notes
with a flag added to the stem.

Two or more eighth notes are written

To count eighth notes, we divide
each beat into two parts, calling the
2nd part "and."

Eighth notes are played twice as fast as quarter notes.
Quarter notes are played twice as fast as half notes.

SHORTNIN' BREAD

MERRILY WE ROLL ALONG
(Duet)

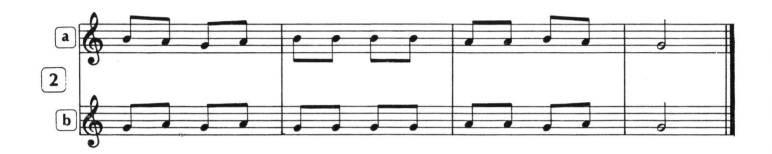

LIGHTLY ROW

DOWN TO LOW E

STUDY IN CO-ORDINATION

Musette from Anna Magdalena's notebook*

J.S. Bach

*Anna Magdalena was J.S. Bach's second wife.

TEMPO SIGNS

Tempo means how FAST or SLOW a piece is played.
The three principal signs are:

Andante *(slow)*   **Moderato** *(moderately)*   **Allegro** *(fast)*

VILLAGE POLKA

Moderato

NIMBLE FINGERS

1st Time — **Andante**
2nd Time — **Moderato**
3rd Time — **Allegro**

ALPINE SONG
(Duet)

Swiss Yodel Song

Moderato

UP ON THE HOUSE-TOP

Moderato

Up on the house-top rein-deer pause, Out jumps good old San - ta Claus;

Down thro' the chim-ney with lots of toys, All for the young ones, Christ-mas joys.

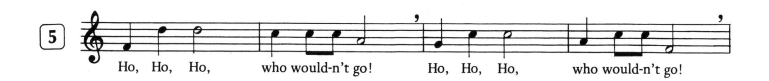

Ho, Ho, Ho, who would-n't go! Ho, Ho, Ho, who would-n't go!

Up on the house-top, click, click, click, Down the chim - ney with good Saint Nick.

LOW **D**

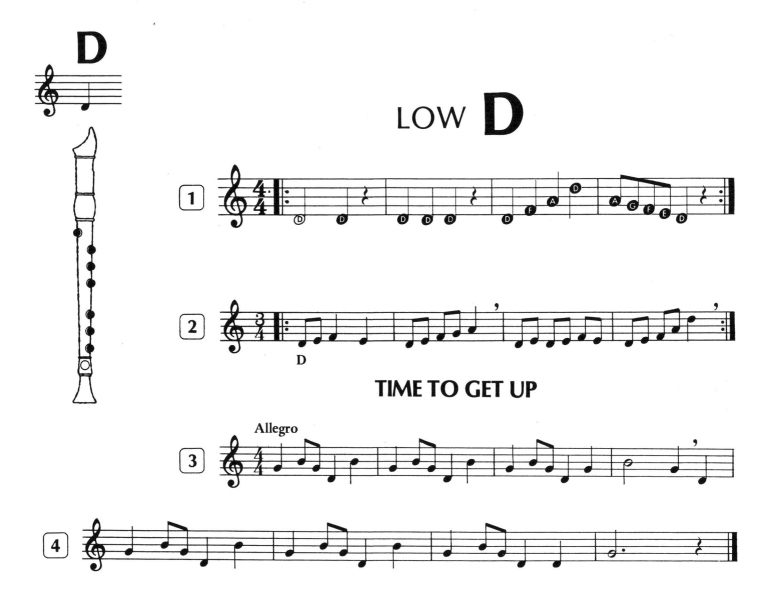

TIME TO GET UP

SWING LOW, SWEET CHARIOT

5 Andante
Swing low, sweet char - i - ot, Com-in' for to car-ry me home!

6 Swing low, sweet char - i - ot, Com-in' for to car-ry me home! I

7 looked o-ver Jor - dan and what did I see, Com-in' for to car-ry me home! A

8 band of an-gels com-in' af-ter me, Com-in' for to car-ry me home!

INCOMPLETE MEASURES

Every piece does not begin on the first beat. Some songs begin with an incomplete measure called the UPBEAT, or PICKUP. If the upbeat is one beat, the last measure will have only two beats in $\frac{3}{4}$ time.

$\frac{3}{4}$	upbeat	whole measure	whole measure	last measure
	3	1 2 3	1 2 3	1 2

CARNIVAL OF VENICE

One beat pick-up

1.

2.

RED RIVER VALLEY

2 beat pick-up

3. From this val - ley they say you are go - ing, We will

4. miss your bright eyes and sweet smile, For they

5. say you are tak - ing the sun - shine, That has

6. bright - ened our path - way a while.

BIG ROCK CANDY MOUNTAIN

1 beat pick-up

7. On a sum - mer day in the month of May a cow - boy came a hik - ing, down a

8. shad - y lane through the su - gar cane he was look - ing for his lik - ing. As he

9. roamed a - long he sang a song of the land of milk and hon - ey, where a

10. man can stay for man - y a day and he won't need an - y mon - ey.

21

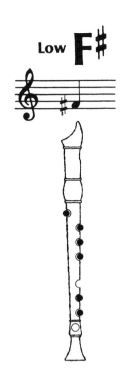

Low **F♯**

The sharp sign (♯) is a symbol used to make a note sound higher.
On a piano, the ♯ means to play the next key higher (black or white).

The sharp sign ♯ affects every other F in the same measure.

O COME, ALL YE FAITHFUL
(Adeste Fideles)
(Duet)

The Christmas Carol was created in Italy in the 13th century. Credited to the monks of the Order of St. Francis of Assisi who sang the story of the Gospel, the carols spread to France, England, Spain and Germany. The French Noel and the English Carol appeared in the 15th century. This hymn was sung in the 13th century but was not transcribed until 1841 by F. Oakeley.

O come all ye faith-ful, Joy-ful and tri-um-phant, O come ye, O come ye to Beth-le-hem. Come and be-hold Him, Born the King of an-gels, O come, let us a-dore Him, O come, let us a-dore Him, O come, let us a-dore Him, Christ the Lord.

(ROUNDS)
DONKEY ROUND

The ROUND, developed from the 14th century ballads called ROUNDEL or ROUNDELAY, is a short melody, taken up by several voices at different intervals.

When the sharp sign (♯) is placed on the F (the 5th) line, it is called the KEY SIGNATURE, and means that every F throughout the piece is to be played sharp.

ROW, ROW, ROW YOUR BOAT
(Trio — 3 Parts)

TIED NOTES

Notes of the same pitch (the same sound) tied together by a curved line

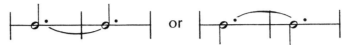

are TIED NOTES: "tie" the beats of the 2nd note to the first note.

DOWN IN THE VALLEY
(Duet)

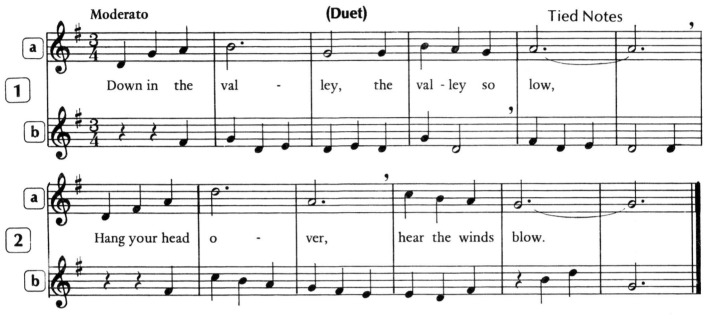

Down in the val - ley, the val - ley so low,

Hang your head o - ver, hear the winds blow.

WHEN THE SAINTS GO MARCHING IN
(Duet)

Oh, when the Saints go march-ing in, Oh, when the Saints go march-ing in,

Oh, how I want to be in that num-ber, When the Saints go march-ing in.

(Natural sign ♮ — cancels a previous sharp for that measure)

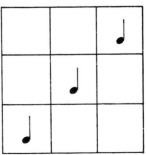

MAGIC BLOCK PUZZLE

Write one note in each block so that the notes across, down and diagonal (except the diagonal line of printed quarter notes) add up to four beats. Use quarter notes and half notes.

MERRY WIDOW WALTZ
(Trio)

Andante

Franz Lehar

DOTTED QUARTER NOTES

A DOT placed after a note increases its value by ½.
We have had the dotted half note:

The dotted quarter note is equal to a quarter note tied to an eighth note:

PREPARATORY DRILL

1 The only difference in the following three measures

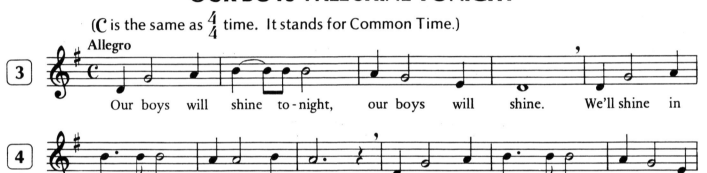

Count: 1 2 & 3 4

2 and these three, is the way they are written. They should sound the same.

OUR BOYS WILL SHINE TONIGHT

(**C** is the same as 4/4 time. It stands for Common Time.)

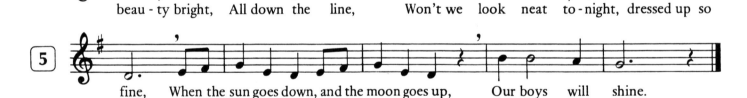

3 Allegro
Our boys will shine to-night, our boys will shine. We'll shine in

4 beau - ty bright, All down the line, Won't we look neat to-night, dressed up so

5 fine, When the sun goes down, and the moon goes up, Our boys will shine.

FAR ABOVE CAYUGA'S WATERS

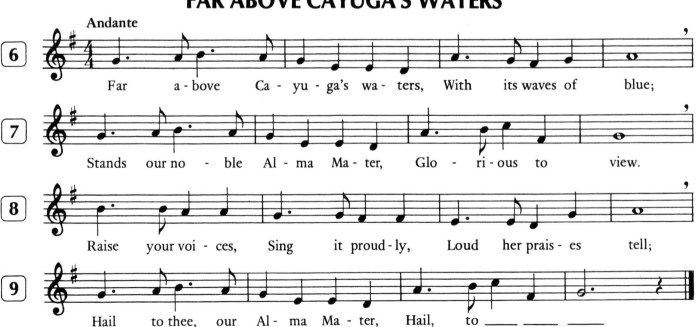

6 Andante
Far a - bove Ca - yu - ga's wa - ters, With its waves of blue;

7 Stands our no - ble Al - ma Ma - ter, Glo - ri - ous to view.

8 Raise your voi - ces, Sing it proud - ly, Loud her prais - es tell;

9 Hail to thee, our Al - ma Ma - ter, Hail, to ____ ____
(your school)

DYNAMICS

The signs of volume (whether loud or soft) are called dynamics:

f — forte, loud
mf — mezzo forte, medium loud
mp — mezzo piano, medium soft
p — piano, soft

MICHAEL, ROW THE BOAT ASHORE

THEME FROM A MOZART SONATA
(Duet)

Crescendo — gradually louder
†Diminuendo — gradually softer

THE STACCATO DOT

A dot placed above ● or below ● a note means to play the note short and crisp.

Think: Tah   tah   tut   tut   tut   tut   tah

HAYDN'S "SURPRISE" SYMPHONY THEME

RAKES OF MALLOW

28

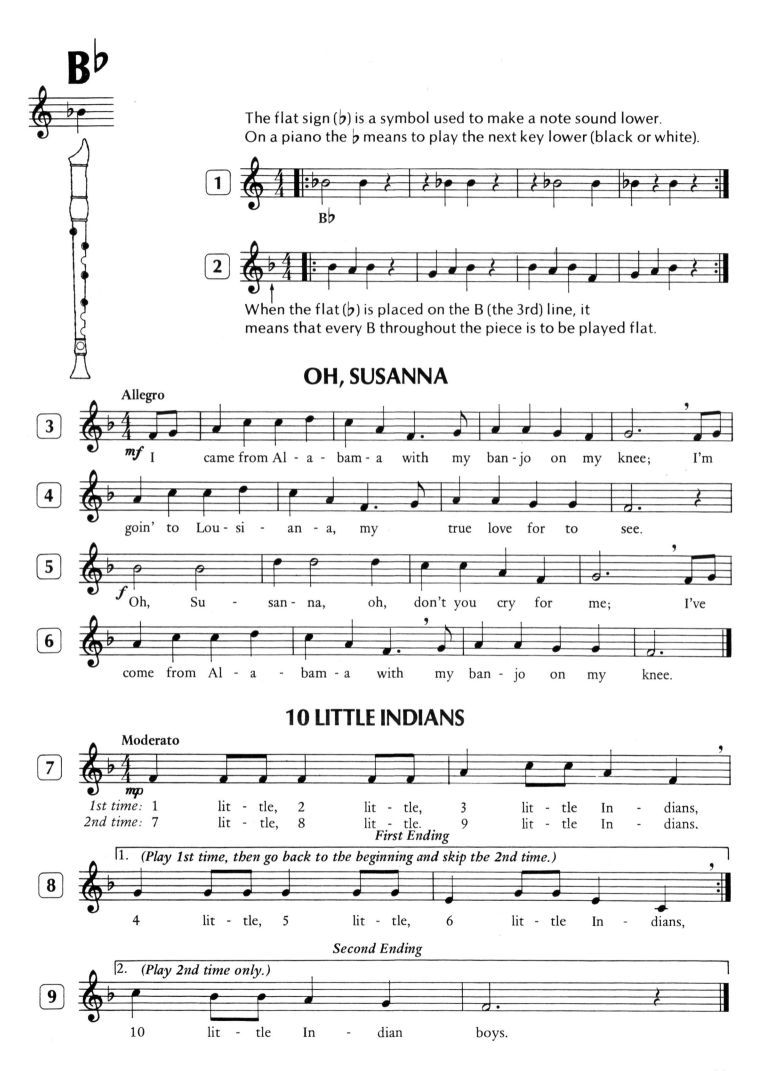

B♭

The flat sign (♭) is a symbol used to make a note sound lower.
On a piano the ♭ means to play the next key lower (black or white).

When the flat (♭) is placed on the B (the 3rd) line, it
means that every B throughout the piece is to be played flat.

OH, SUSANNA

Allegro

mf I came from Al - a - bam - a with my ban - jo on my knee; I'm

goin' to Lou - si - an - a, my true love for to see.

f Oh, Su - san - na, oh, don't you cry for me; I've

come from Al - a - bam - a with my ban - jo on my knee.

10 LITTLE INDIANS

Moderato

mp
1st time: 1 lit - tle, 2 lit - tle, 3 lit - tle In - dians,
2nd time: 7 lit - tle, 8 lit - tle, 9 lit - tle In - dians,

First Ending

1. *(Play 1st time, then go back to the beginning and skip the 2nd time.)*

4 lit - tle, 5 lit - tle, 6 lit - tle In - dians,

Second Ending

2. *(Play 2nd time only.)*

10 lit - tle In - dian boys.

LOW C

LAVENDAR'S BLUE
(Duet)

HYMN from "FINLANDIA"

Jan Sibelius

WAY DOWN UPON THE SWANEE RIVER

Stephen Foster

Fine

D.S. al Fine
(Go back to the sign 𝄋
and play to the Fine)

SCARBOROUGH FAIR

THE FIRST NOËL

The first No - ël the an - gels did say, Was to
fields where they lay keep - ing their sheep, On a

cer - tain poor shep - herds in fields where they lay. In
cold win - ter's night that was so deep; No -

ël, No - ël, No - ël, No - ël,

Born is the King of Is - ra - el.

UP TO E

The thumb hole must be left partially open in order to play the notes from E up. This technique is referred to as ½ hole or pinched hole technique.

BLOW THE MAN DOWN

OLD MacDONALD
(Duet)

From here on, no breath marks are included. Breathe where appropriate, without breaking the melodic flow.

THE SLUR

A SLUR is a curved line that connects notes of different pitch. Tongue the first note only.

THE VICTOR'S MARCH

STREETS OF LAREDO

ANOTHER TIME SIGNATURE

Cut Time (Alla Breve) = ₵

₵ means $\frac{4}{4}$ time cut in half or $\frac{2}{2}$. $\frac{2}{2}$ means 2 beats in a measure, 1 beat for each half note.

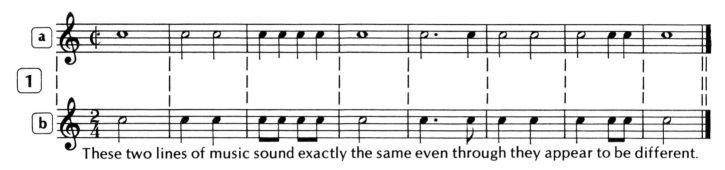

These two lines of music sound exactly the same even through they appear to be different.

HIGH SCHOOL CADETS

J. P. Sousa

THE CAISSONS

SIXTEENTH NOTES

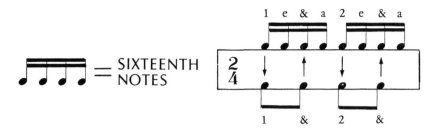

To count sixteenth notes we divide each beat into four parts.

LISTEN TO THE MOCKINGBIRD

BLUE BELLS OF SCOTLAND

THE DRUNKEN SAILOR

(Duet)

MORE SIXTEENTH PATTERNS

UP TO F AND G

High **F** High **G**

WE GATHER TOGETHER
(A Thanksgiving Hymn)

Moderato

C#

AMERICAN PATROL

F.W. Meacham

March tempo

SHIFTING C'S

Andante

rit. = slow the tempo down gradually
a tempo = return to the original tempo

DOTTED EIGHTH FOLLOWED BY A SIXTEENTH

O TANNENBAUM

JOY TO THE WORLD

ST. ANTHONY CHORALE

(Duet)

Franz J. Haydn

*A fermata ⌢ means to hold the note longer than normal.
 It should be held approximately twice as long or as long as you want.

HIGH F#

SWEET BETSY FROM PIKE

ALOUETTE

EIGHTH NOTE TRIPLET

A TRIPLET is a group of three notes indicated by a *3* above or below them ♪♪♪. In $\frac{2}{4}$, $\frac{3}{4}$, or $\frac{4}{4}$ time, an eighth note triplet is played in one beat and equals 2 eighth notes or 1 quarter note.

MARCH from AIDA
(Duet)

NOBODY KNOWS THE TROUBLE I'VE SEEN

A

STREETS OF LAREDO

ANGELS WE HAVE HEARD ON HIGH
(Duet)

$\frac{6}{8}$ TIME

In $\frac{6}{8}$ time there are six beats in the measure and an eighth note is the unit of beat.

POP GOES THE WEASEL

WHEN JOHNNY COMES MARCHING HOME

SUMER IS ICUMEN IN
(Round)

Old English

POMP AND CIRCUMSTANCE
(Duet)

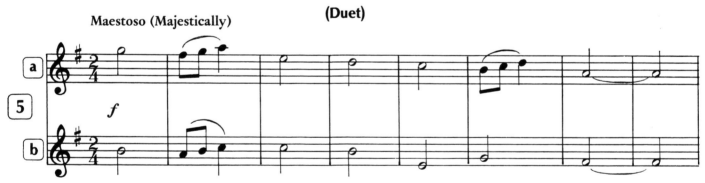

OUR DIRECTOR MARCH
(Duet)

Note Chart for the Soprano Recorder

● CLOSED HOLE

◗ PARTLY CLOSED HOLE

LEFT HAND

THUMB	●	●	●	●	●	●	●	●	●	●	●	●	●	●	●
1st FINGER	●	●	●	●	●	●	●	●	●	●	●	●	●	●	
2nd FINGER	●	●	●	●	●	●	●	●	●	●	●	●			●
3rd FINGER	●	●	●	●	●	●	●	●	●	●			●		

RIGHT HAND

1st FINGER	●	●	●	●	●	●	●				●		●		
2nd FINGER	●	●	●	●	●			●	●		●				
3rd FINGER	●	●	●	◗		●		●	●						
4th FINGER	●	◗				●			●						

↑ German fingering ↑

LEFT HAND

THUMB	●				◗	◗	◗	◗	◗	◗	◗	◗	◗	◗
1st FINGER		●		●	●	●	●	●	●	●	●	●	●	●
2nd FINGER		●	●	●	●	●	●	●	●	●	●	●	●	
3rd FINGER				●	●	●	●	●	●	●				

RIGHT HAND

1st FINGER				●	●	●	●			●		●	●	●
2nd FINGER				●	●			●	●			●	●	●
3rd FINGER				●		●						●		
4th FINGER									●					

↑ German fingering ↑

48